Come
Sail with Me
into a Sea of Poetry
by May F. Lindsey Reed

Come Sail with Me into a Sea of Poetry

ISBN 0-9747-1895-2-0
© Copyright April, 2004
May F. Lindsey Reed
Nashville, Tennessee

Published by

LightHouse Press

P. O. Box 281375
Nashville, Tennessee 37228
lighthousepress1@yahoo.com
615.300.1195

Dedicated to

my husband, Norman
and son
Norman LaMont Reed
[Doctor of Jurisprudence]
my whole family
and
in memory
of
my daughter

Lynnette Fran'za Reed
Miss Black Tennessee 1988
[Killed by a repeat DUI Offender - November 6, 1993]

We pray the young man, who negligently took her life that morning; driving on the wrong side of the highway and alcohol content .24, has sincerely sought rehabilitation through the counsel we learned he was receiving when we went to his first parole hearing, and hope he is now living a worthwhile, productive life. Forgiveness is not difficult when Jesus is at the stern; when Jesus is your guide and compass.

There is a time and purpose for everything under heaven.
We must believe that her time
had been completed here on earth
on November 6, and her purpose was fulfilled

by, through and in Christ Jesus.
And her time was one score and ten years
and seventy-six days.

My heart will be eternally grateful to God for allowing me
to have those precious years, and days of joyous pleasure
and fulfillment to be mother to such a vibrant, generous,
and loving child who told me years ago
"You should write a book, Mama."

Table of Contents

Introduction

I have written from many wonderful memories, thoughts
and imagination. This collection of poems and writings
have been written over the past twenty-eight years. Most
are fictional but many are non-fiction. As a child I read
the volumes of Grimm's Fairy Tales housed at the
Muncie, Indiana Public Library as well as most every
other fictional volume there. The stories were fascinating
and I would tell these stories to my sister and brothers,
and other kids in the neighborhood. Sometimes I'd
embellish a story with a bit of my own imagination.
I feel, however, the real beauty in writing is often that
which is truth.

A short preface is written for a few to capture a better
picture of my thoughts, especially of my childhood, for it
was good, wholesome, pleasant, spiritual and lots of fun.
I hope it will bring a smile, laughter, or cause you to hum
a little tune after reading some of my poems and maybe
even feel like skipping. I have always felt as though
I hold a little bit of heaven in my heart and Praise God!,
I have always wanted to share that treasure with others.

Stories, pictures, poetry, prose, rhyme and verse allow us
to go places, be and do most anything we can imagine.
I've traveled near and far, and done a million things in
my dreams and daydreams as you'll find in my poems.
I shed a few tears of joy over having completed this vol-
ume. May it leave warm thoughts in your heart.

Preface

I don't suppose there is another
literary phrase that's been more
quoted "It was the best of times,
it was the worst of times" but it
is still quite a true and useable
statement. This phrase has run
through my mind many times over
the years and even today as I write
this preface.   I have always loved
reading good literature/poetry and
would, like many of you, memorize
the works of some authors.

It was so much fun writing "Finian's Rainbow."
During rehearsals I'd jot things down in a little
notebook. Just before the last performance I
presented each cast member with a copy. The
expressions of delightful surprise and exclamations
of appreciation was wonderful.

My life has been good. Growing up in Muncie,
Indiana and graduating, 1959, from Muncie Central
High School was great, "Purple and White, fight!
Fight!" Yes, I'm a Bearcat. We won more State
Basketball Tournaments than any other school.
I don't recall the coach's name but Principal, John

Paul Huffman, was a really nice guy. He was friendly and the students liked him.

I won't bother to walk you over the years of my life but, I am filled to overflowing with holy gratitude for each day I have lived. I feel really, really good that I too, now, have a volume of works to share with other readers and poets.

Come Sail With Me
Into A Sea of Poetry

I got into a little boat and
sailed away from shore.
I needed time alone
for my thoughts and words to store.
Oh the air, the space,
the time and place
worked like a Cotton gin.
It started my mind a turning
like the windmill in the wind,
sorting out my many thoughts
as my poetry journey began.
I quietly settled down
for my heart to freely soar.
I sailed and sailed for days on end,
non-stop and wanting more.
I looked above at a clear blue sky –
gray-white sea gulls flying high.
I coulda stayed there forever
for I could feel and see
my Jesus was nigh
and sailing with me.

Come join me now in my little boat –
docked in the corner of my mind;

or set sail in your own
little craft and prepare to fully dine.

Written Tue., September 9, 2003

Draw the anchor now and launch out.
Set your sail to taste, smell, feel, see
and enjoy the full breeze of this poetry sea.
So,
bon voyage and
have a nice sail, mate.

Color Me With Love

My poetry isn't Black!
My poetry isn't White!
It's no particular color
but for people, through God's eyes
seen all alike.
There are poor of every color
in all the land;
color never held a monopoly
on feelings
pertaining to any man.
All pain is painful,
and all tears look the same,
and whenever I hear laughter
its sound is happy
whomever from it came.

My soul never thought of
black words or white
though I know there's many differences
and prejudices to fight;
but somehow my pen flow's free
for this is the way
God gives words to me.
Blood is the soul of all humankind;
the life of all flesh

in Black and White you'll find.
I'll paint this world with words
gathered from above –
They're splattered all around me
singing…"Color me with LOVE."

Written July 6, 1979

I Reckon: My grandfather, Kennon Scott, had a habit of saying "I Reckon!" For a little girl, eight years old, when I first met him, to be answered "I Reckon" nearly every time I asked a question – made this stick in my mind. I reckon God knew it would.

I RECKON

God made me
but I reckon I make Him tired.
God loves me
and I love Him
but I reckon His love for me
is much greater
than the love that I show Him.
God helps me
but I reckon the little help
I give Him is
rather disappointing.
God keeps me
but I reckon I just
keep Him busy.

God wants me to love, care
and share with my neighbor
and never stops hoping that
I'll learn to do so
but somehow,

for some reason,
every time I think I'm
about to get started
doing what I ought,
there seems to be one thing
or another

that gets in the way.
God will never
give up completely on me
though I reckon He gets
pretty mad
and I reckon I'm glad.
You know I reckon if He did
it would really be too bad.

Written summer of 1992

'Tis Worth

Gallant, valiant, stout-hardy
men of old,
fought and died for favor – gold –
sometimes neither
worth their bold;
lost name, fame and gain,
I'm told.

Had any sought to take the time
to learn to live a life sublime;
then lived in fullness
rich and rare,
issuing virtue and love
abundant, fair….
their birth, their life,
'tis worth, 'tis worth.

Written Fri., October 8, 1976

GOD CAN

He languished in poverty many years,
yet met each dawn with laughter – tears.
'Twas not enough through all his trying,
found one brisk morn his sweet love dying.

Coming swiftly to her side he bowed,
and lifting eyes to God he vowed
"If thou but spare my love for me,
of all you ask I'll do for thee."
And as she lay there pale, so still,
his mind, his soul,
suppressed a chill.
But then she stirred,
she gripped his hand.
This gentle soul
loved much this man.

She sensed the fear
that clutched his heart.
She felt the love of God impart
unto her husband's weary heart.

It gave her strength to feel him seek,
thus sent within her breast a peak.
Much more she sought to rise and see,
new hope implored inside with glee;
for now he too had met the Lord,

in ecstasy
brought forth reward.

This healed her tired
and wounded soul,
caused not by life but burden old.

Yes, age and time
and work, and grief;
his finding God gave sweet relief.
Like fetters loosed
from round her heart,
her soul gave leaps to life's new start.

In beams of joy walk they
hand-in-hand.
Only God can change
a natural man.

Written Sat., October 9, 1976

TAKE THE TIME

In years gone by this nice word
"Gay"
was simply not used
in this distorted way.
My meaning is quite
unequivocally clear,
as most well know and must adhere.

Pause in your mind and
turn around.
Try putting this kind of
terminology down.
So many are mixed up,
troubled.......confused;
Don't even realize the words
they misuse.

If we really want to get ourselves
set right,
get the Bible and concordance,
let biblical education
lead the fight.
Learn of the word,
find this conclusion;
in avoiding
reality and truth,

leads one to ill illusion.
Like the drawing of shutters
across the mind;
though still living and breathing,
like a grave you'll find
that to waste and not want
to learn more of the Master,

can render your
life a total disaster.
Christ is the way!
He'll make your life "GAY!"
I mean joyous and happy
and placed in array.

So children,
read, love, learn and discern.
Cease to trifle, ridicule
and squander,
but read to discern
every word that you learn.

Written Wed., November 10, 1976
[Literarily speaking –only]

11

Shun-Nough Will: An illiterate, Dixieland mother of meager means and little strength or energy is trying to draw out the thoughts of her son as he hasn't begun to show any interest in his life nor made any effort towards helping or improving himself. She senses that it is possible he may eventually realize the need to start thinking about his future and she is sincerely inquiring of his thoughts and plans.

SHUN-NOUGH WILL

"MY CHILE,
HOW DOES YA SEE THINS?"
"I see's lots,
but liddle of it makes much sense."
"WELL WHAT DOES YA THINK
ABOUT WHAT YA SEE'S?"
"I don't bother thinkin bout it much."
"IT SHOWS!
WELL HOW DOES YA FEEL?"
"Don't feel much a anythin."
"NOT MUCH ONE WAY
OR ANOTHER, HUH?"
"Yeh, dats rhet!"
"WELL DOES YA PLAN
TA DO ANYTHIN
WIT YA LIFE?"
"Don't rhetly know rhet now.
Anyways, I ain't gonna take da time
rhet now ta worri bout it;

worri makes me tir'd an I is tir'd
nough already from doin round
dis hare house."
"BOY, YOU'S DON'T KNOW
WHAT IT IS TA BE TIR'D.
YOU'S DON'T KNOW WHAT
IT IS TA DO;

YOU'S DON'T KNOW WHAT
IT IS TA REALY WORK
AND LAWD KNOW
AT DIS LATE DATE
LESSEN SOMETHUN MIGHTY
POW'RFUL HAPPENS TA
GETS YA STARTED –
YA AIN'T NEVAH
GONNA KNOW."
"Awh Ma, I is tir'd nough already.
Does I have ta listen ta all
dat talk you's always spoutin?"
"NAW BOY! YOU'S GO ON;
SOMETHUN GONNA BE
HAPNING TA YA ONE OF
DESE DAYS....
YOU'S WAIT! YOU'S SEE!"

Written Wed., February 2, 1977

13

REMEMBER

There were Saddle Oxfords
and white Bucks; remember!
Lots wore Penny Loafers and
thick bobby sox's; remember!
There were pony tails
and spit curls; remember!
Girls wore long flared skirts
and boys – mostly white shirts;
remember!

Black leather jackets
and pegged blue-jeans,
the hippest threads,
Kool! Real keen!
Heads shaved so close
you called it peach fuzz,
and I'm not kidding,
that's the way it was;
remember!

Those sock-hops in the
old school gym
were plain outa sight.
You'd want them to go on forever,
all night;
remember!

Yes, those were the 'good old days'
carefree and gay.
Your folks would tell you,
"it won't always be this way!"
It would bug you
ever time they'd say it;
remember!
We'll never forget those
'good old days'
we'll just
carry on….. and remember.

[Do you remember the 50s?]
Written Fri., March 18, 1977

Because God Is... You Are!

I was not, and now I am.
I did not know, I could not know.
I did not know I knew not
And then I knew I knew not.
I learned and then knew,
and knew that I knew.
Seasons came and went.
I stretched upward and out.
My shadow grew long.
My head towered high above the earth
of whence before I'd toddled close.
My chin's smoothness grew rough.
The tendons of my limbs flexed
and filled of brawny flesh;
there was no longer a boy –
but a man.

Sensing my strength,
yet needing not to prove it,
I walk softly;
I speak not thoughtlessly to
or about anyone.
I reach out in love to others
and seek reproach in no man.
If misunderstood
I strive to calmly explain
or if rebuffed – to

quietly walk away with a
gentle whisper in my heart....

"Remember who and whose you are,
what you are, · why you are."
In my soul His Spirit answers
"Yes, because I AM... you are!
Walk softly young man.
Walk in My Way."

Written Sat., June 7, 1975

Night: My pastor, Bishop Tom Benjamin, in his message one Sunday morn, was saying how some folk just don't like the night; that they really don't like to turn out the lights at night and be in the dark........that they'll think of one thing or another to hinder them from dealing with the darkness. Well I like the night – when you leave off from doing; the phone stops ringing, no one knocks or rings the door bell, movement outside dies down to a minimum and when you lie down and everyone is still you can hear the beautiful silence and sounds of the night – like a cricket rubbing modified parts of his fore-wings together creating a chirping melody. And on a clear night you can see all the stars and illustrious celestial elements in the heavens. Or when the moon is full it casts a soft iridescent illuminating glow upon the night which gives you a feeling almost as though you were walking in a dream. The night is very special, so restful, peaceful; a time of quietude and renewal for the mind and weary flesh.

Night

The night slips down like a wet,
inky blanket of velvet black;
dazzling diamond studded with the
illustrious, unmatchable elements
of His universe.
I gaze upward into the

endless ebony velvet,
stretched over all my eye can see.
I feel if I but reach out my hand that I
might touch it – but no, I mustn't.
It appears that I might disturb
or alter this utter magnificence.
Such exquisite contrast
from the day.
Day—night—I love them both.
In night I am left off from doing.
I hold no anticipation of an unexpected
rap or ring;
nothing to split my quiet thoughts.
My heart sings, it leaps, it soars.
It is soothed at the end of day
by the coming of night.

I lie calm;
my time to be still,
to refill and replenish my soul.
This night is good,
is sweet,
is mine.
My soul speaks,
the Spirit listens;
He hears, He knows,
He feels my seeking
and is there for me.
Our spirits meet in His temple
and I rejoice.

As I lie beneath this mystical
blanket of absolute pure blackness
I marvel at my creator's talent.
The world is a good place to live!
In truth –
the world is the only place to live.

Sleep cometh;
how restful the hour
and quiet the night.
His calming blackness
awaits my slumber.

Written Wed., January 19, 1977

Pins, Balls and Fun

There goes a ball,
another and another;
it's 'Light of the World'
bowling with their brother.
League members many –
some old, some new,
lend warmth and laughter
to the Meadows bowling crew.

The style of each bowler is their own,
let's say – unique;
and bowling or watching
relays a fine treat.
A bowler steps forward,
he eyes the pins,
finds firmly his footing
and then his ball sends.
He holds his position
as he watches it roll,
sucks in a deep breath –
will he render his goal
to split and splatter the pins
from their place,
leaving nary a one for his ball to face?
Hank Crews stands poised, turns,
faces his team,
a smile so big,

showing confidence in Gleem.
And duly do,
as he'd certainly tried,
everyone of those pins was
lain on its side.
Lots more make strikes
and spares –
no less,

Ed Brents can tell you,
they all will confess.
Each team tries its utmost
and gives all they've got.
The team with most points will
rise to the top.

Though only one will surface
ultimately winner;
they alone will not celebrate,
the whole gang will have dinner.
So share you must
and continue to be
the most Christian organization
Circle City could ever see.

Written Sun., February 6, 1977 [Non Fiction]
[The Meadows Bowling Alley is now defunct]

Springtime

Springtime is the sweetest time of year I know.
It holds the most anticipation of things to grow;
the flowers, the plants, the billowy trees,
the grass, the butterfly and little old me.
Each morning bursts forth with a
thrust of sun.
Its rays of warmth sweep down to run.
It spills and splashes its beams of light;
seeps right inside me to my delight.
I bask in its warmth and slide open
my mind
to brilliance and splendor and
skip through time.
I slip to its solstice –
then return to sing;
my mind travels swift and fastest in spring.
A fresh April shower pops open a bud;
cat and dog shake off their mud.
Birds fly from housetop to tree,
content in their
dwelling with friends like the bee.
A magnificent rainbow half circles the sky;
I watch till it fades and nod a goodbye.

The sun shines brightest now,
most nearly noon;
by and by it bends, dips westward –

my mind then flips to June.
What lies ahead for me –
my thoughts whirl round my brain?
What awaits me this new summer –
will it be loss or gain?
My thoughts reach up to a setting sun,
almost reverse to the way it'd begun.
Radiantly relaxing
in a gleaming, golden, coral sea;

how warm, how sweet how lovely –
right fetching to me.
The clouds cast shadows
lean and high;
seems smelted right against
a pale heliotrope sky.

Night approaches to paint its black,
like a mountainous woven
spider spun flax.
Ah – I sigh,
its been a beautiful day;
yes, simply beautiful
in most every way.

Written Tues., February 22, 1977

Sweet Knowing

Amidst our clamorous times,
the valor of true souls chime.
Like a Peace Rose, sweet,
laboriously clinging to the melody fleet.
Lean thee unto gales of charity;
lifting life's most precious prosperity
until He whispers
"Will you come hither to me?"
Thus we blossom hereafter, evermore,
endlessly –
with the Master.

Written Wed., October 6, 1976

A Child

I like to run! I like to play!
I like to be happy!
I like to be gay (keenly alive)!
But sometimes I sulk – I sit and stare
and I get real mad and I don't care.
I make mean faces
and frown and frown,
and I don't even want my best friend around.

Then mom says,
"Go to your room and take a rest."
I kick and pout and spoil the test…
that's to see if I've learned to be
at my best.
I lie on my bed facing the wall;
oh how I feel so very small –
I don't like being by myself at all.
Now what had made me act so rotten?
Gee! by gosh! I've quite forgotten.
Well it doesn't matter now but
just the same,
I'd like to find someone else to blame.

I slip off my bed
and touch lightly the floor;
I open so softly to look out my door.
I sneak down the hall

to peep in the kitchen;
if Mom catches me
she'll say I'm a vixen.
I tiptoe lightly across the floor;
I lean and stretch to try and see more.
I feel a soft and gentle hand
but it startles me so
on my bottom I land.
I look up in Mom's face
and she's smiling at me;
she's just the best Mom ever you see
and she'll never stop loving me
however I may be.

Written March 1, 1977

Dishes And Wishes

She steps in the kitchen
about a quarter to four;
She prepares a meal that would seem
quite a chore.
It's warm and cheery and all aglow –
like counting Peanuts for Mama –
you know!

Now we've just finished dinner,
my was it good.
Mama sure can cook,
that's most tastily understood.
Those dishes are now staring,
looking solemn and bare.
I'd like to ignore them,
just leave them right there.
But Mama would call
or come to my room
and if she sent Daddy
my fate would be doom.

So I'll scrape them and stack them,
being careful and not crack them.
I'll wash them all clean,
then rinse and let drain.
The water that's left I'll blot
with a towel;

I'll place in the cupboard
then take a small bow.

All washed, dried,
and put in their place,
just look at me,
I'm on top of this race.
I'll be back at the sink tomorrow,
to my displeasure,
and to my sorrow.

Sometimes I wish we didn't eat
and didn't have to be so neat,

and didn't have to do the dishes
but spend our time on other wishes.
Just fun and play and having a ball;
not any worries – no none at all.

But I surely know
what Mama would say
and I don't want to hear it anyway;
so I'll continue to do the dishes
and push out of mind
my foolish wishes.

Written Tues., March 15, 1977

29

'Twas A Dream

Sometimes I dream,
I go far and wide.
I travel through moments auspicious,
I glide.
There's a real grand time
to be sought and found,
from mountain top
to a swinging playground.

I can sit on a throne
with scepter in hand
or switch to nomadism
and roam through the land.
Then suddenly I find myself
the world's greatest star;
making fabulous movies
is the best by far.

The bell is rang! all horses break to run,
I'm a Jockey now and boy is this fun.
Standing on the bottom of the sea
with Swordfish
and Octopus is spectacularly free.

WOW! the clouds are so fluffy and white;
being a stunt flier is just
plain 'OUTA SIGHT.'

I'll zoom straight up and try
a triple twist;
then make a sharp dive
and spin as though a disk.
'Tis plenty of
pleasing pleasure I'll treasure,
Tho none of it real
but it did seem;
No none at all
but 'twas a dream.

Written Thurs., March 17, 1977

Take Thought

Have you ever sat and listened long
to find then nothing said?
Have you ever pondered
deep and hard
if you'd something missed with dread?
You wonder how you'd heard so much
and yet you'd heard so little,
like lifting high into the air
an almost empty kettle.

For lengthy speeches
sometimes teaches
seldom much is taught,
when length, not worth,
is dwelled upon
with absence of a thought.

Written Fri., May 20, 1977

Try Child

Sometimes things seem to weigh you down;
too many decisions
and so many things to do
but you say – "I'll try!"
And often it's hard to talk to anyone,
to make them understand
but you decide – "I'll try"
and when you do
you question whether or not
you should have and if you've maybe
made things worse
and you think – I may as well just give up;
then again you say,
"no,
I'll keep trying!"

Day after day you really see no way of things
getting better.
You don't want to give up
and with that same thought – "I'll try!"
you lift your head, you fold your hands,
you bend your knees and you pray.
You know God is there,
that He hears, that He cares,
that He answers prayer.
You tell Him all about it…
and you thank Him way down deep inside.

He tells you
'everything's gonna be al-right –
to just hold on; to trust and believe.'
You feel so much better
and speak right out loud
"I'll TRY LORD!"
and you feel as though
you actually hear him answer
"That's all I ask child, is that you try."

Written Tuesday, March 22, 1977

Finian's Rainbow: This Broadway production was performed at the Christian Theological Seminary Repertory Theater in Indianapolis, Indiana in the Spring of 1977. For my audition I sang 'Climb Every Mountain' and landed a part in the show as a singing sharecropper. The songs were all so zesty and alive. When we began rehearsals I would write excerpts of things happening and comments made by cast members. Corbin Patrick, writer, with the Indianapolis Star, attended the Sunday evening performance on May 8. He wrote an article about the show which was in the Tuesday paper on May 10. In my poem I included a line from his article. I had copies of my poem printed on paper the colors in the rainbow and on the night of our final performance I presented a copy to each member of the cast. Everyone was elated to receive it, especially those I had included a personal comment or gesture. The Director, Loretta Yoder, was noticeably surprised and touched. This was a sweet memento for every-one to take with them. We did seventeen shows with nifty little things being added here and there. I can't remember having had more fun.

Finian's Rainbow

From the very first day we began to rehearse
I listened and tried hard to remember each verse.
The notes weren't really necessary for me,
but the timing, the words, the songs' melody.

A sweet pleasant smile would
come through the door,
stride to the piano and smile even more.
She'd call our attention the chatter to end,
touch lightly the keys our lyrics to blend.
It took a while, success sometimes slow,
but definite promise began to show.

Our director so sturdy, studied and sure,
gave poise, with confidence, and added allure.
Taking our places down on the stage,
choreography with song did lend new sage.
Some dancing, some singing,
few doing both at first;
but to master the dilemma expelled a
new thirst.

Time and again the same mistakes,
while being pointed out
afforded small breaks.
Scenes being called exposed
faces of dismay,
"left or right, my God which way."
A blunder here, a stumble there,
pauses a few too many
but Loretta yelled,
"You're doing fine, by opening night
there won't be any."
"Yeah" said some "right" said others,

we all felt pretty darn good.
And duly so, this was our show,
we clearly understood.

The orchestra transformed sent forth
tantalizing new sound.
It lent zest and zeal as we all rushed around.
Well slowly things began to take shape.
I relaxed more now
but continued to tape.

The day soon came when
all the show was set.
We even had our costumes;
now this was a sight, you bet.

May 5 we opened like a Morning Glory
and Tuesday, May 10,
Corbin Patrick wrote the story:
"Lovely, lively, cheerful and bright"

in short, sheer pleasure, real joy,
sweet delight.

The show moved along ever so swiftly,
little things being added
made it really quite nifty.
Then it was over,
all those fun days were gone;

the singing and dancing
in my mind lingers on.
And in my heart the memory lives dear.
The many new faces
remain fondly, so clear.
I'll remember this wonderful show
through the years;
a show with a heart,
filled with mirth and love – you know.
Your show and mine!
our "Finian's Rainbow."

Written May 15, 1977
Non-fiction

A man that hath friends must
shew himself friendly:
and there is a friend that sticketh closer
than a brother.

Proverbs 18:24 (KJV)

Pre-Adventure

How often does a lovers heart
mean words the lips may utter;
when found a lie the soul doth cry
and bringeth forth a shudder.

A stifled love is hard to bear,
affection is a need.
Ambivalence settles in the mind,
quite threatening indeed.

Be wise in choice, your life ensure.
Good looks do not a life make pure.
A broken heart for some will mend,
while others heartache never end.

Hereafter seek deep to find;
prerequisite is there to line.
Knowledge brings the wise
much more
and helps make life the less a chore.

Written Thurs., May 26, 1977

Eye See

The eye is the mind's delight;
a window to the soul.
Let in some light,
send out some light.
Let us dole, and dole, and dole.

Lift high the window,
your life excel.
Let peace, with harmony,
transcend, propel.

The tongue shouldeth not
the eye to crowd;
through seeing much,
speaketh not too loud.
Daunt quick the lips, the vain,
the proud.
Shed ever thoughts
that make a shroud.

Written Wed., June 1, 1977

Ali: In 1959-60 there was a friend of mine, Junie
Hall, who boxed in the Golden Gloves. He was good
and was really excited about boxing that year in
Chicago. He was matched with the young boxer,
Cassius Clay, and was beaten. That young man later
changed his name to Muhammad Ali and went on to
become the World Heavyweight Champion. I never
had the opportunity to meet 'Cassius' or Ali but I felt
kinda like I had met him from the way Junie talked
about him. Junie said to me, when he returned home
from the fight, "Cassius is good! He's just a better
boxer than I am." His loss stayed on his mind. Junie
was really a very good boxer too; I told him so.

Ali

In my coming and my going
I've learned of
some men's station in life.
I have found some
to truly stand tall
and others who thought they did
but didn't really at all.

I've found some who dearly desire
to excel
but through lack of preparation or
determination,
continue to fail.
And then there is one,

though not always right,
'I'll follow my heart, I'll win
and I'll fight.'

Well fight, yes he did,
with heart,
mind and word.
Whenever he speaks there've been
many who've heard.

I've seen his story, it was great,
yes -- it was grand.
It told so much about Ali the man.
He's 'Great', though not 'The Greatest'
only God can be...
I'm talking about the man
Muhammad Ali.

Written Tues., June 21, 1977

Boxing Ali

Smooth, clean-cut, a boxer indeed.
No slugger, he just punches;
clean, fast, with zest, with speed.

His dancing delightful,
is charmingly sprightful
and all would agree,

if they were like me,
that he's simply "The greatest"
this boxing Ali.

Countless vicissitudes in life
has his been.
With intrepid wit
he's met each one to win.
When military decisions
streamed his way;
he held fast, thought deep,
he leaned but didn't sway;
He said "No, I won't go!
At home I'll stay."

His emolument
from much hard work increased.
Chattering, tattling
from time did cease.

He remains the same,
untouched by gain.
May much more goodness
from life to him rain.

Written July 1, 1977

43

Would I?

Would I have stood with Jesus
some 2000 years ago?
Would I have spoken out loud
to let the people know?
Would I have helped if I could
and would I have felt that I should;
would I?

Would I have just watched
their foolish state,
their spitting, hissing, cuffing, hate?
Would I have spoke out
to plead His case;
would I have had courage
to stand face-to-face?
Would I have pointed at Pilate and said
"not this man but Barabbas
is the one to be dead"
would I?

Would I have objected
as they led him away?
Would I have spoken yet more that day?
Would I have denounced
those evil men of Rome;
Would I have pushed them aside and
tried taking him home;
would I?

Would I have dared reach out
to grip
the hand that held that
dreadful whip;
the hand that scourged my Lord so dear
or would I have stood in silence, fear?
Would I have dared
rebuke the crowd;
their screaming, jeering, piercing, loud –
their ugly taunts from their
menacing tongue'
or would I have trembled
and nothing done;
would I?

Would I have used force
as they led him to the hill?
Would I have rushed to stop them,
not stood scared and still?
Would I have slapped the
tools from hand
as they pounded the nails
into this man?
Would I have trampled the
crown of thorns,
thrown it aside – not let it be worn?
Would I have flung the
vinegared sponge aside –
knelt at his feet,

steadfast to abide;
would I?

And when the sun refused to shine,
would I have known then, this Lord,
He was mine?
Would I have raised my head and cried
"not He Father,
some other should be tried?"
And when He spoke those
few last words,
would I have listened,
would I have heard?
"Father, into thy hands I commend my spirit:"

Would I have felt then
all was lost?
Would I have realized the priceless cost?
Would I have known
though He was dead
He'd rise again as He had said?
Would I have let gloom
possess and bind?
Would I have known then
He'd made salvation mine;
that He would rise on
"Resurrection" morn
and leave the world no more forlorn;
would I?

I doubt if I'd have known that day.
I doubt if I'd had much to say.
I doubt if I'd done anything at all.
I doubt if I'd have answered
if He to me did call;
and yet today as we rejoice,
of those who heard and knew his voice;
Peter, James, John
and all the rest –
they watched my Lord go through
this test.
They watched in fear,
in anguish, shame;
afraid to speak their Master's name.

But then at morn as Mary came;
her heart so heavy;
too filled with blame.
She found the huge stone rolled away
and sat there angels
more bright than day.
"He is not here, but is risen."
The grave no longer held him prison.
Resurrected by his Father on high,
now men
no more need fear to die.
Amen.

Written June 21-22, 1977

18 And they all cried out at once, saying, "Away with this man, and release to us Barabbas" —19 who had been thrown into prison for a certain insurrection made in the city, and for murder. 20 Pilate, therefore wishing to release Jesus, again called out to them. 21 But they shouted, saying, "Crucify Him, crucify Him!" 22 And he said to them the third time, "Why, what evil has He done? I will therefore chastise Him and let Him go." 23 But they were insistent, demanding with loud voices that He be crucified. And the voices of these men and of the chief priests prevailed. 24 So Pilate gave sentence that it should be as they requested. 25 And he released to them the one they requested, who for insurrection and murder had been thrown into prison; but he delivered Jesus to their will.

Luke 23:18-25   [NKJ]

Et Demain
[and tomorrow]

When I last breathe and am no more,
my soul set sail on a bright
new shore;
then take my body,
throw it away;
I'm no longer there –
I've gone home to stay.

Now don't you fret
and don't you cry;
I am not dead,
I did not die.
I'm just resting till that great day
and hour
when all God's children
will blossom like the flower.
Then once again,
but in a better time and place;
Ma-ma will smile
to see again, my child,
your face.

Written 1970's

A Poem of Love is about my pastor, Bishop Dr. Thomas Garrott Benjamin, Jr. I wrote it during the time I was working as Membership Secretary/ Receptionist at my home church, Light of The World Christian Church, Indianapolis, Indiana. Dr. B., as we affectionately called/call him, arrived each morning with gusto. He is a very energetic and innovative individual and I decided to write a poem about him. I began to make notes of some of the things he would say or do. He is real and genuine and naturally unique and it didn't take long for me to have quite enough data to write this poem.

Dr. B. made most every day an adventure and shared his unbounded enthusiasm with everyone around him; then and now. He loves people and people love him. He has the ingenious quality of being able to compose and present God's word very uniquely and effectively. Bishop Tom Garrott Benjamin, Jr. is an exceptional man of God. He is has been Senior Pastor at Light of The World Christian Church since October 1969.

God's Exceptional Man
A Poem of Love
Written In Honor of
Reverend Dr. T. Garrott Benjamin, Jr.

He bursts' thru the door so zesty and vital;
never a moment for being lazy or idle.

"Well good morning girls!
How are you today?
you all look so lovely – I really must say."
He spills compliments neatly,
sweetly and discreetly,
then bounds up the hall
to start the day;
always on the go! yes, this is his way.
Buzz-zz-zz; "How about a cup of tea!"
OK, sure Dr. B.,
but must you have it so sugary?
Now his secretary marvels
at the brilliance of her boss
but shakes her head
his desk to see
displays a total loss.
The radio plays softly –
when a tune he'll fancy
brings him down the hallway
to do a little dancy.
"What do you think of that"
he'll say;
"I'll bet you didn't know
I could move that way."
Comments small, not too many,
but the Staff Secretary
generally
doesn't have any.
He teasingly makes note

of her fewness
of word;
being careful he'll not be
considered a nerd.
Spinning quickly around on the
balls of his feet,
he sometimes encounters the
Book Keeper to greet.
"Good morning Dr. Benjamin,
you're looking rather fit;
you know the busy life you live
leaves not much time to sit."
So Reverend Dr. T. Garrott Benjamin, Jr.,
my friend;
this busy life should never end.
And when you travel,
preach, sing and pray –
remember fondly
of this day;
of many a face, song and voice
you've heard
and know God smiled with every word.
Keep holding his unchanging hand.
Yes, God has truly touched this man.

Written Fri., night as it stormed –
September 30, 1977
This poem was shared with the congregation
in a service honoring Dr. B.

Reverend Dr. Alvin O'Neal Jackson had served as a student minister at Light of the World Christian Church while attending Butler University in Indianapolis, Indiana. He later was called to pastor the Loudon Avenue Christian Church in Roanoke, Virginia. He returned to The Light as Associate Pastor in 1977. He, like Dr. B., is one of the most talented and genteel young ministers in America. This poem, too, was shared with the congregation. On the evening of the celebration I asked if he would inject the words "This is good!" himself, as this was something he often said/says. I just had to include it, and what could be better than having him speak the words.

Dr. Jackson has been Senior Pastor of the National City Christian Church in Washington, D.C. since April 1, 1998. He served as Moderator of the Christian Church (Disciples of Christ) for 2001-2003.

Reverend Alvin O'Neal Jackson

He has been here before,
some seven years ago.
He left his mark and he left his glow.
Then a short time back –
Dr. Benjamin, with congregation,
sought this man.
To the Light he came quickly
to aid, yes, to stand.

When he left he was alone
but returned with a mate;
she is lovely, so gracious,
I'd say it was sweet fate.

Example is the message he shows each day;
always caring – this is his way.
Now his favorite expression,
and if he would...
Reverend Jackson – will you say it
"This is good!"

Yes, good indeed that you and I
should have a friend who says
"I'll try ."
Genteel, well-bred, refined
and polite;
a specimen for God
and a pure delight.
We all here applaud
our satisfaction,
for not fraction but ACTION
is the word for
Alvin Jackson.

Written thru love - 1977

Reverend Henry M. Williamson

He came bustling into Indy –
hardly anyone knew his name.
Took pastorate at Phillips Temple,
thus 'twill never be the same.

Known now in our community with
PUSH –
he's on the go.
He's really special people,
here at the Light we know.

The first time I met him
and much to my surprise,
he reminded me of my Pastor
with that twinkle in his eye.
Stretched out his friendly hand to shake,
placed mine in his
and friends did make.

I've not known him long,
don't know him well
but of what I know I'll write—I'll tell,
for it's men such as he
that cause hearts to swell.

Keep striving Reverend Williamson,
this life not always filled with fun;

but with the precious few like you
we others learn to follow, to do.

The world needs more
like you and yours,
to preach God's word
and open doors.

Yes we at The Light embrace our
new found friend;
hence together, through Christ,
help us others to win.

Written Circa 1979

Be Still And Know

The wind so high I could not sleep,
I pulled back the curtain
to take a peek.
These words flecked within my mind
I turned toward my desk
for a pen to find
and here on the pulp
I placed each line.

Looking out upon a flurry of white;
my world stands still,
my heart is in flight.
O the beauty and fear I grasp with a smile,
not much I can do,
I'll just be still;
I'll rest a while.

May - be man races,
rushes too much about.
May - be God saw need to slow him down,
no doubt,
And I'll be still,
I'll rest a while.

Billowy, pillowy snow-mounds are spun.
The fierce wind-gales
rend their fun.

There goes a gust,
twirling and twirling,
billions of flakes jubilantly swirling,
but I'll be still;
I'll rest a while.

Something utterly magnificent,
wondrously omnipotent
to gaze upon
a nostril's blast,
then see for days
how long 'twill last;
so I'll be still –
I'll rest a while.

Written Thurs., January 26, 1978
as our blasting blizzard began-Indy.

Rhapsody In Truth

As the sun rises and sets,
blessings are showering upon you.
God's ever present love
is there to strengthen.

Give thanks for the
years that have passed.
Take Christ, each day, with you
and help goodness last.

Don't fret of wasted hours and days,
but run on swiftly
in righteous ways.
Reach out with a smile,
grasp life as a child.

Of happiness and truth
receive freely in youth
for too soon is the
symphony ended.

Written Summer of 1978

In Sooth

Wedded lavishly, luxuriously,
thus at length;
resplendently set in the hour.
Love leaping,
illuminating passions' power.
But stood there in the shadows
a lady of woe,
She'd often shared his bed.
Tears spilled over the rims of her eyes
as she heard words
he'd often said.

More tears streamed down the walls
of her heart;
she ached at the sight of these two.
A lump grew large within her breast,
she did not know what to do.
Their lips touch,
gently they embrace;
she longed to rush forward,
their fingers unlace.
She sighed deeply, yearningly,
then quietly slipped away,
as this picture held hurt and
anguish this day.

Time exposed harsh truths
to this lady of woe
as she cradled her troubled heart.
Her love having taken another that hour
tore and splintered her world apart.
Deemed suave, elite,
a real man about town;
by his family, thought 'oh, the best'.
But neither impression
would aptly describe
this man of growing detest.
The two viewed quite sweet,
did seem perfectly unique
but 'twas not the case, indeed;
for he being adulterate
did regularly alternate,
hence sifting their splendor to seed.

The lady of woe thought
"no, no,
no longer so"
to cherish dreams
which might have been;
but grew stronger and richer
in joy of wisdom –
for her transgressions
had reached an end.

Prayed she for he
of only surface worth,
may one day come to know;
then love abound when faith he's found,
the Master's grace bestow.

Written September 1, 1978

Born Again!

Nature is the surest
and by far the sweet and purest
for all it gently touches in the Spring.

The Deity sends a warming breeze,
caressing all below.
Feathered friends – chirp, chirp-chirping
letting all creation know.

Burnt brown grass proclaims "I'm green!"
flowers quietly bloom.
Bee and butterfly flitter – sip, sip – sipping,
tasting from nature's master loom.

The earth lay pregnant
these past few months,
swollen full and still;
She brings forth now abundant birth,
she joyously doth yield.

Written Sun., March 18, 1979

I'm So Sorry

.....and now –
what will my future be?
I've let men steal my best from me.
What is there that I can say?
I've left my love and my beauty
in embraces stray.
I feel all my worth has been wasted.
I've allowed myself to be used.
I feel so tired, foolish, drained, abused.

Why wouldn't I listen when friends
tried to tell me my lifestyle
could destroy me?
I don't know why I've lived this way!!!
WHY – DIDN'T -- I -- LISTEN!?
I never stopped to think about
my lifestyle
until it was too late;
so busy trying to have a "good time"
and I'd just date and date.

What was I looking for?
What did I think I needed?
So beaten now, worn, tired and sick,
I'm lonely, wretched and defeated.
My life –

how I rue it.
Trying to be cute and cool,
I became a total fool!
None of my "Friends" come visit anymore.
No one rings the telly
or knocks at my door.
I'm weary and sorry
and so ashamed
and I really have only myself to blame.

My life's been reduced to nothingness,
a mere disgusting pitiful mess.
I lie here and miserably weep;
such pain to shut my eyes for sleep.
Ma-ma comes quietly through my door,
I know she loves me
but greatly deplore.

My thoughts keep darting
here and there,
the pain offends my flesh.
Thoughts tumbling, twisting,
turning, and turning…
inside my mind whispers – hush!
An early grave!?
Oh my God! I'm sorry –
I'm so sorry!

Written February 9, 1980

Miss Eva Jean Wrather: The epitome of the word
"Historian." It was a privilege and honor to meet
and come to know this extraordinary woman who
was a Founding and Charter Member of the Disciples
of Christ Historical Society which is the library and
archivesof the Christian Church (Disciples of Christ),
independent Christian Churches and Churches of
Christ and is located in Nashville, Tennessee. As a
scholar and writer she was an authority on the life
and ministry of Alexander Campbell, the most promi-
nent of the Four Founding Fathers of the Christian
Church. She spent the greater portion of her life
researching and writing about him. Held in high
esteem by the entire fellowship, she stood in a lofty
position within the church, in the annals of the
Historical Society and in the hearts of the people.
Her work, gifts and talents will be remembered
and hailed by generations.

The library and archives of the Christian Church,
prior to being moved to the Vanderbilt campus
in 1952, was, at its inception, housed at Culver
Stockton College in Canton, Missouri. Miss Eva
Jean was present for the groundbreaking and laying
of the cornerstone in 1956. This lovely Tudor-Gothic
structure was completed and dedicated to the glory
of God in 1958.

The Historical Society honored her in 1991 and I wrote this little poem-thought for that auspicious occasion. I have, since then, rewritten a portion of it as a memorial to Miss Wrather when she was again honored by the Historical Society on Sunday, June 22, 2003, in the naming and dedication service of the Eva Jean Wrather Study Room. A grand reception followed. It was held in her former home, 4700 Elkins Avenue, where she had lived her entire life. Eva Jean departed this life, Thursday, September 13, 2001.

Eva Jean Wrather
Disciples of Christ Historical Society
A Founding/Charter Member

She helped make
1956
a most momentous date.
She beamed in its completion in 1958.

She helped to
bless the building for all it meant to
be, by sharing with her life and dreams
the things her heart could see.
It is only well and
fitting as we gather here this day,
to say "well done"
Eva Jean, and

"thank you!"
You were a leader all the way.

Written November 3, 1991
Adaptations April 2003

Whatever thy hand findeth to do, do it with thy might;
for there is no work, nor device, nor knowledge, nor
wisdom, in the grave, whither thou goest.

Ecclesiastes 9:10   KJV

My Sister Loretta

My sister, my pal, my confidant,
and friend;
you're one whose been with me
through thick and thin.
Our hearts and lives are entwined

through love —
the kind that's learned from
our Father above.

There are miles between us
but our hearts
never apart.
Linked deeply with love
like a horse to a cart.
Sometimes I'm pulling with you
in the cart
But more often you're pulling;
you have so ooo oo much heart.

We're missing our mother now
whom we both loved so dear,
but we have remembrances
filled with joys
and with tears.
This gift of life has been bitter and sweet

and our sisterhood has remained
deep and unique.
No squabbles, no meaness,
but real love and esteem.
Like a rose in a garden
you've tended with care;
no wonder my heart bends,
always ready to share.

I love you so much Sis!

Written June 1999
[Non-fiction]

That Day!

The sun rose,
as always,
from the blackness of night;
September 11 was dawning,
the day took flight.
Its rays stretched bright across the sky;
many awakened from slumber
like you and I.

Some started with coffee, juice,
a song or a sigh,
not wanting this day either
to pass them by.
Shaved, showered, shampooed
and dressed;
most, surely feeling confident,
good, and blessed.

No one suspected what was coming
in that hour;
only God – Father and Son
in their Holy Infinite Power.
For others had prepared to threaten,
maim and kill;
to take lives and joys in a way that
seemed unreal.
But Lord, don't let us fret too long.

Let us pray for one another that we
might be strong.
Time will heal every woe and care.
This, Jesus has shown us and will
help us to bear.

Blessings surround us
in a myriad of ways;
we need only to yield,
recognize life's each phase.
No woe is so great that God cannot
attend.
God's love and grace
will always descend.

Written Thurs., October 4, 2001

A Maiden – A Man – A Savior

She was just a young girl
as pure as a pearl,
had a beau whom dearly she loved.
They planned to be wed,
and then heavenly led in a life sweet as doves.

But it seemed at this point
that that couldn't be
and she listened, she wondered
and waited to see;
for an angel Divine,
brought a message sublime;
thus she prayed and waited to see.

It's a blessing to know
God will certainly show
His will and the way we should go.
For Mary, dear sweet Mary,
so young and betrothed,
experienced absolutely no woe.

Joseph, too, met the angel
and was told the good news,
for he first was filled with dismay.
But learning the truth
from the angel divine,
put his mind in wondrous array.

How the shepherds rejoiced,
how the angels did sing
at the birth of the Savior, our King.
Wise men crossed the wide plain,
they came from afar;
they followed a bright shining star.

Christ brought the world worth
as Mary gave birth,
all heaven and earth stood in awe.
For Jesus, Lord Jesus
had come forth like the wind,
to bring and to give His great law.

Written Mon., December 3, 2001

Just Transitioning

Got up this morning just running
around.
I finally said "stop!" and sat myself
down.
I was all out of breath when I got a
HOT FLASH.
I scolded myself while letting it
pass.

I talked right out loud as I fanned my
face,
chided myself on slowing my
pace.
Getting older and changing can be rather
hard;
before you get started you're feeling
down-right tired.

I'll just keep myself busy;
my mind and my
heart.
I won't let me be lazy,
it wouldn't be smart
although sometimes – it feels – things are coming
apart.

I remember the saying

"you're as young as you feel."
Yes, this is true and
life is so ooo oo
real.
I don't doubt now,
that I'll keep getting
older,
but God and His Word
will just make me
bolder.

Written Thurs., January 10, 2002
[non fiction]

A Call To Worship

Coming together, coming to worship,
coming to give thanks.
Coming to lift up Christ' name,
coming to share Christian fellowship,
coming to sing, coming to read God's Word,
coming to witness one to another,
COMING TO PRAISE OUR LORD;
Come rejoicing!
And come we must,
bringing the many varied attributes
of our lives
that attribute to God's existence
in this world and in us.
Bring your smiles, your tears, your songs,
your joys, your sorrows,
your hope in this day
and for all your tomorrows.
Bring all that you have to the
Throne of Grace.
Release all that you are and receive
all that you need...
come believing,
come giving, come receiving;
COME GLORIFY GOD!

Written in the mid 90's
[See first entry-] The Gifts We Bring: Worship Resources for
Stewardship And Mission, Volume 3
Church Finance Council - Christian Church (Disciples of Christ)

Mankind's Mindset

Mankind is filled with knowledge,
of this we overflow.
But of true wisdom, understanding,
few in this life doeth show.

Men today judge others by an
acquired or earned degree.
Some simply lack the wisdom that
would help set man's soul free.

We've learned all the proper phases,
laboring through life's different stages;
we practice daily what to say
and worry forever if folk think
we're okay.
Blessings pass by day-by-day
when we lack God's word
or fail to say
the simple truths that make us strong,
those truths that help
our life prolong.

Unlock the door of mind
and heart.
Let God's word enter and peace
impart.
Enjoy life, the world, and all that's

been given.
Deny the ways that make life driven.
Deny the Satan that grips, that rivets,
for Jesus came, died, and now
"Is risen!"
No!
Satan cannot hold the mind,
the soul prison.

Written Mon., April 15, 2002

Do's, Don'ts, Needs And Wants

Don't run too fast,
don't fly too low,
keep your eyes and ears open
wherever you go.
Learn to adjust to life's turns
and bends.
Don't run with a crowd
but find a few good friends.

Show kindness, thoughtfulness,
use the common touch.
Don't stay out too late
and don't talk too much.
Often it seems difficult to know

exactly what's best.
Every little task seems to be
some sort of test.
Simple hello's feel like a chore,
and things unexpected
are a nuisance,
a bore.

Life's daily routine gets tedious, mean;
while everything and nothing
seems to fit in your schemes.
You want to do this

but you need to do that;
things get too jumbled;
you want to throw in your hat.

So all of your do's,
and all of your don'ts,
all of your needs,
and yes,
all of your wants,
they build, and build, and build, and build;
your heart is made heavy, jaunt.

But then you hear that
still small voice
that calms your thoughts and fears.
That sweet and gentle
comforting voice
that drives and dries the tears;
Un huh,
it drives away all fears.

Written June 28, 2002

'Twill See You On Yonder Shore

Now wasn't that a humdinger of a dream;
and at this time
what does it mean?
Old friends stopping by
just laughing and talking,
said they were getting lazy so they
went out walking.

Well they must have walked for a long,
long time,
since we live in the present
and they live beyond sublime.
But as long as God lends
memory to mind;
and as long as we remember loved ones
and like kind;
we'll see them and hear them
in our thoughts most everyday.
And we will see them again,
truly,
as God has made a way.

Written August 28, 2002

82

So – Who's The Child

You really find it hard to believe,
some folk worse than simply naive.
This old race has suffered a
major breakdown
where parents often ask the children
and the children put down.
Put down mama, daddy,
uncle and aunt
and when asked to do something
give a threatening "I ain't."

Well that's not the way God meant
for things to be.
No, not hardly, surely you must see.
I wonder how things got so
turned around;
children doing the bossing –
parent(s) being a clown.
Everywhere folk mixed-up,
things out of place.
'tis a shameful display
like a slap in God's face.

And many, one day, will look back
and say
"If I'd made Jeremy mind –
I wouldn't be paying this fine"

or "If I had talked to my Greta
she would have known better"........
"If I'd chastised my Fred
he'd be alive, not dead."

Parents, teach them now while
they are small.
Discipline now
or later – not at all.

Teach them what's right,
to shun the wrong.
Teach them uprightness
that they might grow strong.

Written September 5, 2002

My son, do not despise the chastening of the Lord,
Nor detest His correction; For whom the Lord loves
He corrects, Just as a father the son in whom he
delights.   *NKJ Proverbs 3:12*

Correct your son, and he will give you rest; Yes, he
will give delight to your soul.   *NKJ Proverbs 29:17*

When I Was A Child

When I was a child we made our own fun
and oh what fun we made.
When I was a child there was so much to do
and so doing much we did.
When I was a child we stayed busy and playful,
we never took much time to complain.
When I was a child
we enjoyed the little things,
most everything caused passionate exclaim.
I was lively and active,
I loved to skip, run and play.
Not to skip and play made for a miserable day.
We played kickball, softball, Mother May I,
and jump rope;
Dumb School, Hop Scotch, Red Rover
and Simon Says.
Dodge Ball, Leap Frog, Hide and Seek.
We played jacks, checkers,
ran relay races
and walked on stilts.
We high jumped, pole vaulted,
scooter and roller skated.
Made Push Carts, played Tag,
Red Light Green Light and Crack the Whip.
Boy oh boy....wow!
It was just so much fun being a child.

I'm glad I was a child when I was a child.
Enjoying one's life when young
makes all the difference
in the world.
My childhood thoughts and memories
are all unfurled.

Written Wed., September 25, 2002
[non-fiction]

Have You Ever

Have you ever experienced
a heavenly day
where you felt lofty and bright,
springy and light;
and things felt just right
in your heart, in your sight,
and you just felt good,
not at all uptight...
no fights to fight –
just serenely alright?

It is moments like this that
sweetens the soul.
It is moments like this
that you just want to hold.
It is moments like this that
should be shared;
should be told.
It is moments like this that
make you feel whole.

Written Fri., August 30, 2002

Life Means Adjusting

Life is just livin
each day you're givn,
not worrying about the rest.
Life is a mystery,
soaked deep with history;
life should be lived at its best.
Life will certainly make manifest
what's good, what's bad, what's raw.
So you deal with things
as best you can
and there's moments that'll
cause you to bawl.

But the world just keeps turning,
nothin stays the same;
life certainly has its ups and downs.
If you learn to turn with it
and lean in the curves,
you'll enjoy just being around.

In this coming New Year
why not plan to do
what's good, what's best, what's wise.
Share "HIS Word"
rich and sweet;
help lift the lonely,
lost and bleak
and wondrously open their eyes.

Written December 19, 2002

It's Raining
[When I Was A Little Girl]

On a hot, rainy, summer day
when the sun was
shining bright and all shimmery,
I would think
'oh how beautiful!'
The rain, wet and refreshing
was so nice;
wet, wet, wetter than most anything
and better than a bath
cause you didn't have to
take time to soap a cloth.
I would slip off my shoes and go
walking in it.
I liked the way the soft gooey mud felt
squishing between my toes.
It was really fun and you
wouldn't have to wash your feet
because the rain cleaned them off.

I would hold my head back
to feel the rain
splattering on my face,
trickle down and tickle the
back of my neck.
I would get soaked through and through
and would have great fun

splashing in most every puddle I'd see.
The sun so bright would begin
burning me
and I'd run and run and
feel free as could be.
Life should always be as sweet and
pleasant as my
childhood, rainy, summer days.

Written Wed., January 15, 2003
[Non-fiction]

My Horse

God fashioned the horse,
He whispered; declared,
I've made you sleek and strong
for great work you've been prepared.
Your joints and tendons made firm
with strong sinews,
for there'll be much
and strenuous labor
fashioned for you to do.

My greatest creation
will mount upon your back.
You will quickly adjust and
accept this fact.
You will walk with him, carry him
and work day-by-day
and at times you'll just run free,
frolic and play.
Some will be ever so gentle and amuse
while others, insensitively
may strike, whip and abuse.

I've given you a temperament of
calm perception.
You'll respond to gentleness,
love and affection;

with keen smell, hearing, sensing danger
and direction.
With sinewy gracefulness and elegant style,
high nickers and whinnies that'll
linger a while.
Gallop free, unrestrained,
much strength you possess.
Toss high your head my wind will caress
your face, your mane,
your magnificent frame;
loving all my creation and
none are the same.

Written Tue., February 25, 2003

Sounds of My Choo-Choo Memories

Whoo whoo, whoo whoo,
Choo choo choo choo, choo choo choo choo,
whoo whoo, whoo whoo,
choo choo choo choo,
choo choo choo choo.

As I prepared for bed up in my sister's room
last night.
I heard the whistle of a train;
it brought back memories like a light.
I thought of all the days gone by
when I was still a child.
It started when that whistle blew
and lasted quite a while.

Not a scenic view – our neighborhood,
this was certainly a fact,
for we lived only a block
from the
rambling railroad tracks.
We crossed them more than once
in a day,
sometimes walking the rails.
It was a challenge to balance,
I must say;
it was fun, it was pleasure, it was play.

We loved to watch the trains pass by –
we'd wave at the Pullman Car.
We knew the many passengers inside
had come from near and far.
The train would rumble and rattle,
never quiet but always loud.

Whenever Conductor
blew his whistle in our presence,
he audienced a children's crowd.
The pretty red caboose
would slowly fade from sight.
Oh how I love the whistle of the
Choo Choo Train,
especially in the night.

The clickity clack clacking
from the shifting of the cars
beat out a nifty rhythm –
helping me sing unwritten bars.
The whistle and the rumble and thoughts of
days gone by
makes me feel real good inside
and sometimes makes me cry.
Whoo whoo, whoo whoo,
Choo choo choo choo, choo choo choo choo,
choo choo choo choo, choo choo choo choo.
Whoo whoo ooo.

Written Monday, April 7, 2003
(Non-fiction)

My Life

First I am nothing; at least not unto where one finds
pleasure in me. I am somewhere living peacefully,
resting carefree and happy when these terribly irritat-
ing, rude and menacing creatures come and take my
family and me away from our beloved home. We are
tossed to and fro – just every which way. Finally,
when we think, ah, it is all over, we are tossed about
even more. We are moved about excessively but at
length our destination is reached. These creatures put
us through a grueling, horrendous process that leaves
us in small flattened strips, and very stiff. They dress
us in different colors and designs, then send us to
places unknown to us. As these creatures will always
have their way – we are placed where we are easily
accessible and many of them come and take us in
hand. They lift us, look us over and by the exchange
of strange objects, the creature who always guards
the area – lets them, one-by-one, take us away.
They slide off our heavy coat and remove our pre-
cious silver lining. They shove us into a small dark
cave where we are senselessly battered and bruised.
There is a great pink flap inside which obnoxiously
bullies and pushes us about. There are many differ-
ently shaped shades of white stones that clamp down
repeatedly on us to prevent our escaping. We are
badly beaten and bitten by these oddly shaped jagged
stones. There is a frightening ravine at the rear and

some of us are very nearly shoved off into it; truth-fully, a few have reaped their end in that bottomless ravine by the onerous, merciless, disgraceful antics of that cruel, meaty, careless pink flap.

After a time these creatures tire of torturing us. Some fling us from the cave, sending us flying against cold or hot surfaces. Never thinking to be kind and con-siderate enough to put back on our warm silver-lin-ings – and so, there we lie, molten, helpless, home-less, dirty, lonely and alone.

They say "There Are Twelve-Million Stories In the Naked City. This has been one of them." This is the story of my journey into life – the life of a stick of chewing gum.

Written April 4, 1958

Some of you may remember the old black & white television movie series "The Naked City" which I have taken the quote from. It was a great favorite of mine and most folks I knew when growing up. I would watch it still – if it was aired. It held a great human-interest thought for the viewers. I thought it was simply the perfect way to conclude this writ-ing. ©

Dem Dere Ole Tornadoes

It wus jus lik da sky had busted open an all
dat water in da clouds jus come spillin out.
Almost lik den da wind decided ta git involved
an started stirrin da rain roun – da way a
top spins, an afore ya knew it it done got
so wound up dat de only way it could stop
wus tah rush down an burro itself intah
de earth – but it jus done got its speed so
built up dat it took mo den two or three
times a burroing itself cause jus once couldn't
slow it down or stop it, an it jus kept on
goin-long foe quite a spel – once it done got
started.

Moss of da time dem dere ole tornadoes
does a awful lot of damage; an cause dey
gets out of control, sometime folk git hurt
or eben killed, an dat ole wind don't eben
know what it done did. Use ta be – folk
'tweren't so busy rushin round an dey'd
take mo notice of da sky; an dey'd know
bout when da sky was a gonna bust open
lik dat an would git deyself someplace reel
safe – lik a ole cella in de ground. We's got
all dat fanci quipment now ta tell us when
ole 'Brother Wind' is gettin all twisted an
wound-up but we's don't habe dem ole

cellas to climb down intah an let dat ole 'Brother' pass o'va; an we'ens jus gets all smashed up an thrown ever which-way. We's jus gonna habe tah start lookin up an not be so busy doing an gettin heah an dere. Bes way tah see what's a going on o'va yo head is tah look up regalar lik. Jus keep on a-lookin up an da Lord'll show ya tings ya nevah noticed befoe.

We'ens betta start usin sum common sense cause dem dere ole tornadoes don't habe none a-tall. Yeh, betta start usin dat plain ole common sense – whatcha wus born wit.

Written Thursday, May 15, 2003

Mr. Mars and Old Man Moon

Looking up into the sky last night
as I hummed a little tune,
I saw a small red, celestial sphere
just adjacent to the moon.
I stared and stared
and finally thought
'it certainly isn't stars'
and marveled to my little self
if it possibly could be Mars.

I'd never seen this celestial sphere
and stared with growing delight,
as I noted a tinge of blue
and a tiny speck of white.
It really grabbed my attention
so assistance I commandeered
and received a lovely show
as through binoculars I peered.
I've wondered about this planet
whom scientist say is red –
I took one long last stare at it
and shuffled off to bed.
Old Man Moon was a
beaming dark yellow,
really almost brown;
it didn't seem to brother him at all
having Mr. Mars around.

As I awoke next morning
I heard the newsman say
"It was a number of calls made last night"
about that odd solar display.
It had definitely been determined
Mr. Mars had made a show,
while Old Man Moon
kept brightly shining,
reflecting his heavenly glow.

Written Mon., August 11, 2003
This sighting was reported
Wednesday, March 16, 2003.

Well now, if you are here on this page
I think you have finished
reading all my sea worthy poetry.

Sure hope you enjoyed the sail
and found the content of the
sea to be a keepsake
to treasure.

SEE YA NOW!

About The Author

May F. Lindsey Reed is a native of Illinois but grew up in Muncie, Indiana. She confessed Christ, April 9, 1950, and was baptized by the Reverend M. A. Lowe, Pastor of Bethel A.M.E. Church. May graduated from Muncie Central High School on June 4, 1959. She began modeling for The Muncie Camera Club at 17 and enjoyed it immensely. She was later employed with Ball Memorial Hospital as X-Ray Film File Clerk from 1961-1965 before attending the Academy Business College in Indianapolis, Indiana to train as a Keypunch Operator the summer of '65 and began working at Fort Benjamin Harrison Army Finance Center that Fall. In 1977 May performed with the Christian Theological Seminary Repertoire Theater. Later that year she took the position of Membership Secretary/Receptionist for her home church; Light of World. Bishop Tom Garrott Benjamin, Jr. is Pastor. In 1979 she moved to the position of Office Manager. She also served as a deaconess, sang with the Mass Choir and taught the Youth New Members Classes.

In 1981 May moved with her family to Nashville, Tennessee as her husband, Norman, had received his Master of Divinity degree from Christian Theological Seminary in 1980, ordained to the Christian ministry and had been called to the pastorate of the Alameda Christian Church in Nashville. In 1982 she was called to the position of secretary/receptionist at the Grace M. Eaton Day Care Home and was there until May of 1983 when she was asked to come to the Disciples of Christ Historical Society in a like position, and in 1985 she was moved to the position of Assistant Librarian. Through the years her diligent and competent work of research, leading workshops, museum preparations, giving tours, etc., having inspired the Board of Trustees of the Historical Society, honored May, in 1996, naming her 'Docent.' She retired December 1999. She continues to assist at the Society whenever called upon.

May served on the Board of Trustees of the National Convocation of the Christian Church (Disciples of Christ) from 1996 through 2002, and as President of the Ministers Wives/Husbands Fellowship from 1998-2002. May writes poetry and loves sharing the word of God with others.

In 2002 May was asked to take the position of Editor of The Poet's Corner for the African-American publication for Disciples –THE OLDTIMERS' GRAPEVINE by the Editor, Oscar Haynes….May says "Wow, what an honor!"

She is married to Norman Reed and they have one son, Norman LaMont who is an Attorney-at-Law in Indianapolis, Indiana. Many loving memories are held in her heart for her beloved daughter, Lynnette Fran'za, whose life was cut short by a repeat DUI offender. May says "Lynnette's Spirit is always with me". God has touched May in a very special way, she says "I have responded to His touch."